LYRICALL

THE LIFE AND TIMES
OF BERNIE TAUPIN

KEKE ALEXIS

ISBN: **9798854875844**

TABLE OF CONTENTS

INTRODUCTION

Bernie Taupin, a name that resonates with music enthusiasts and fans around the world, is an iconic figure in the realm of songwriting and artistic expression. Born on May 22, 1950, in Sleaford, Lincolnshire, England, Bernie Taupin's journey in the world of music began to unfold with remarkable artistic prowess. He would go on to become one of the most influential and celebrated lyricists of his time, leaving an indelible mark on the music industry.

From his early years, Taupin exhibited a keen interest in literature and writing, which laid the foundation for his future creative endeavors. Raised in a rural setting, he developed a deep appreciation for nature and the poetic beauty of the English countryside, which would later find its way into his lyrical compositions. This upbringing not only shaped his writing style but also fueled his passion for storytelling, capturing the hearts of millions through his evocative and emotionally charged lyrics.

The fateful encounter that would change his life forever took place in 1967 when Bernie Taupin responded to an advertisement placed by Liberty Records in search of songwriters. This advertisement would bring him together with a young and talented musician named Reginald Kenneth Dwight, who would later become the internationally renowned Elton John. Their serendipitous meeting sparked an extraordinary creative partnership that would redefine the landscape of popular music.

Bernie Taupin's story is one of artistic brilliance, resilience, and artistic evolution. It transcends the boundaries of conventional songwriting, touching the hearts of listeners from diverse backgrounds and generations. As we embark on this journey through the life of Bernie Taupin, we will discover the essence of a creative genius whose words have the power to inspire, uplift, and evoke profound emotions, leaving an enduring legacy in the world of music and beyond.

EARLY LIFE AND BACKGROUND

Bernie Taupin was born on May 22, 1950, in Sleaford, a small town in Lincolnshire, England. He grew up in a modest family setting, surrounded by the picturesque beauty of the English countryside.

Taupin's childhood was marked by a deep connection with nature and a profound appreciation for the rural landscape, which would later become a recurring theme in his songwriting.

From an early age, Taupin displayed a love for literature and writing. He was an avid reader and found solace in the world of books and poetry. This love for storytelling and the written word had a significant influence on his future career as a lyricist. The beauty of the English language and the power of words captivated him, leading him to experiment with writing poems and short stories during his formative years.

Growing up in a relatively isolated environment, Taupin found comfort and inspiration in the vastness of nature surrounding him. The idyllic countryside provided a canvas for his imagination, and he often drew inspiration from the landscapes and the changing seasons, incorporating these elements into his lyrical compositions later in life.

As a teenager, Taupin's fascination with music began to grow. He immersed himself in the music of the 1960s, drawn to the sounds of folk, rock, and pop that were making waves at the time. This exposure to various musical genres expanded his artistic horizons and influenced his songwriting style.

Despite his rural upbringing, Taupin possessed an innate desire to explore the world beyond his small town. This wanderlust and curiosity about life outside the countryside would play a role in shaping his perspective and storytelling abilities. His dreams of venturing into new territories and experiencing life's diversity would later find expression in his lyrics, which often reflected themes of adventure, escapism, and self-discovery.

In his late teens, Bernie Taupin decided to pursue a career in art and design. He attended the Regional College of Art in Luton, where he honed his artistic skills and explored different forms of visual expression. This artistic education and exposure to diverse artistic mediums would prove to be invaluable in his songwriting career, as it allowed him to approach lyricism with a visual and imaginative flair.

It was during this time that Taupin saw an advertisement by Liberty Records looking for songwriters. Intrigued by the opportunity, he responded to the ad, showcasing his poetic talents. This decision would lead him to the life-changing encounter with a young and talented musician named Reginald Kenneth Dwight, who would later be known as Elton John.

The meeting of Bernie Taupin and Elton John would become the catalyst for one of the most extraordinary songwriting partnerships in music history. Their complementary talents, shared vision, and creative chemistry would propel them to unparalleled heights of success and shape the trajectory of their respective careers.

Bernie Taupin's early life and background laid the foundation for the poetic brilliance and lyrical depth that would come to define his songwriting legacy. His upbringing in the embrace of nature, love for literature, and artistic pursuits contributed to the unique and emotive voice that continues to resonate with audiences worldwide.

MEETING ELTON JOHN

The serendipitous meeting of Bernie Taupin and Elton John in 1967 marked the beginning of a life-changing partnership that would revolutionize the music industry and leave an indelible mark on popular culture. The two young talents were brought together by fate through an advertisement placed by Liberty Records, which was searching for songwriters at the time. Little did they know that this seemingly routine response to an ad would set in motion a creative journey that would redefine the landscape of contemporary music.

When Elton John, then known as Reginald Kenneth Dwight, received Bernie Taupin's response to the advertisement, he was immediately struck by the depth and emotion in Taupin's lyrics. Elton, a gifted musician with a prodigious talent for piano, recognized the poetic brilliance and storytelling prowess evident in Bernie's words. Despite their different backgrounds and upbringings, they shared a deep artistic connection that transcended barriers, and they soon decided to meet in person.

Their first meeting took place at a modest apartment in London, and it was an encounter that would change both of their lives forever. Bernie Taupin, a reserved and introspective young man with a passion for literature, and Elton John, an outgoing and charismatic performer with a flair for the piano, discovered an immediate bond through their shared love for music and storytelling.

Elton's musical expertise perfectly complemented Bernie's lyrical finesse, creating a seamless collaboration that would become the heart and soul of their partnership. From the moment they started working together, it was evident that they were a musical match made in heaven. Bernie's emotionally charged and evocative lyrics found their perfect melodic counterpart in Elton's captivating piano arrangements and powerful vocals.

Their songwriting process was unconventional but immensely successful. Bernie Taupin would often present Elton John with a stack of handwritten lyrics, and Elton would sit down at the piano, effortlessly composing melodies that breathed life into Bernie's words. Their creative synergy was so profound that they rarely worked together in the same room, yet their music spoke volumes about the deep understanding they had for each other's artistry.

The early years of their partnership saw the rapid rise of Elton John's career, and the duo started gaining recognition in the music industry.

Together, they released a series of critically acclaimed albums, such as "Empty Sky," "Elton John," "Tumbleweed Connection," and "Madman Across the Water." Each album was a testament to the duo's innovative approach to music, blending various genres, and pushing creative boundaries.

One of the most remarkable aspects of their collaboration was the freedom and trust they placed in each other's abilities. Bernie Taupin gave Elton John the space to interpret his lyrics in his unique style, while Elton had complete faith in Bernie's ability to craft powerful stories that resonated with audiences worldwide.

Their iconic album "Goodbye Yellow Brick Road," released in 1973, solidified their status as musical legends. It featured hit after hit, including "Candle in the Wind," "Bennie and the Jets," "Saturday Night's Alright for Fighting," and the title track

"Goodbye Yellow Brick Road." This album showcased the incredible depth and versatility of their artistic collaboration and further cemented their place in music history.

Over the decades, Bernie Taupin and Elton John's partnership endured, producing a multitude of chart-topping hits and critically acclaimed albums. Their contributions to the music industry were recognized with numerous awards, including Grammy Awards and inductions into the Rock and Roll Hall of Fame.

Beyond the professional realm, Bernie and Elton developed a deep friendship that endured through the ups and downs of their careers and personal lives. Their bond as creative soulmates was unbreakable, and they continued to work together on new projects and albums, exploring fresh musical avenues and challenging themselves artistically.

The meeting of Bernie Taupin and Elton John remains an iconic moment in the history of music. It was a fortuitous encounter that brought together two exceptional talents, whose combined brilliance continues to captivate audiences worldwide. Their enduring legacy as one of the greatest songwriting duos of all time serves as a testament to the transformative power of artistic collaboration and the magic that can be created when two creative geniuses come together in perfect harmony.

COLLABORATIVE JOURNEY WITH ELTON JOHN

The collaborative journey between Bernie Taupin and Elton John stands as a testament to the power of artistic synergy and mutual admiration. Spanning over five decades, their partnership is one of the most successful and enduring in the history of popular music. Together, they created a vast and diverse body of work that resonated with audiences across the globe and left an indelible mark on the music industry.

After their fortuitous meeting in 1967, Bernie and Elton quickly established a creative bond that would become the backbone of their musical journey. Bernie's introspective and poetic lyrics found a perfect match in Elton's melodious compositions and impassioned vocals. Their unique dynamic allowed them to experiment with various musical styles and genres, resulting in a distinctive sound that defied categorization.

The early years of their collaboration were marked by a prolific output of albums that showcased their artistic evolution and growth. Starting with "Empty Sky" in 1969, their debut album together, they went on to release a string of critically acclaimed works such as "Elton John" (1970), "Tumbleweed Connection" (1970), "Madman Across the Water" (1971), and "Honky Château" (1972). Each album brought something new to the table, showcasing their ability to craft songs that ranged from heartfelt ballads to upbeat rock anthems.

In 1973, the duo achieved unparalleled success with the release of "Goodbye Yellow Brick Road." This iconic double album became a cultural phenomenon and remains one of the most celebrated works in their discography. It produced timeless hits like "Bennie and the Jets," "Candle in the Wind," and the titular track "Goodbye Yellow Brick Road." The album's popularity solidified their status as musical legends and elevated their partnership to new heights.

As their collaborative journey continued, Bernie and Elton's approach to songwriting evolved. While Bernie's lyrics continued to delve into themes of love, loss, introspection, and societal commentary, Elton's musical compositions expanded in complexity and experimentation. Their willingness to push creative boundaries allowed them to stay relevant and fresh throughout the years.

In the late 1970s and early 1980s, the duo explored new territories with albums like "Captain Fantastic and the Brown Dirt Cowboy" (1975), an autobiographical concept album that delved into their rise to fame, and "The Fox" (1981), which showcased a more electronic and experimental sound.

The 1990s saw a resurgence of Bernie and Elton's popularity with the release of "The One" (1992) and "The Lion King" soundtrack (1994). The latter featured some of their most beloved and iconic songs, such as "Can You Feel the Love Tonight" and "Circle of Life," earning them Academy Awards for Best Original Song.

Beyond their music, Bernie and Elton's friendship played a crucial role in their enduring collaboration. They stood by each other during personal struggles, celebrated each other's successes, and remained committed to creating music that spoke to their shared artistic vision. Their unwavering support for one another fostered an environment of trust and mutual respect, which contributed to the longevity and authenticity of their partnership.

In the 21st century, the duo continued to create music and tour together, captivating audiences worldwide with their live performances. They released albums like "The Captain & the Kid" (2006) and "The Union" (2010), further demonstrating their artistic prowess and unwavering commitment to their craft.

Throughout their collaborative journey, Bernie Taupin and Elton John left an undeniable impact on the music industry. Their songs became anthems that transcended generations and cultures, touching the hearts of millions with their emotive and thought-provoking lyrics. Their ability to tell stories through music, coupled with Elton's dynamic performances, made them a force to be reckoned with on the global stage.

Their partnership serves as a shining example of how artistic collaboration can lead to groundbreaking creations that resonate with audiences for generations to come. Bernie Taupin's evocative storytelling and Elton John's musical genius blended seamlessly, resulting in a body of work that continues to inspire and uplift listeners worldwide. As they continue their creative journey together, Bernie and Elton's legacy stands as a testament to the enduring power of music to connect, heal, and transform lives.

SONGWRITING SUCCESS AND HITS

Bernie Taupin's songwriting success and the array of hits he penned with Elton John constitute a remarkable chapter in the history of popular music. From the moment they began collaborating, their partnership proved to be a powerhouse of creativity, producing an impressive repertoire of chart-topping singles and critically acclaimed albums.

Their earliest successes came in the late 1960s and early 1970s when they released a series of albums that solidified their place in the music industry. Songs like "Your Song," from the self-titled album "Elton John" (1970), and "Levon" and "Tiny Dancer" from "Madman Across the Water" (1971), showcased Bernie's heartfelt and introspective lyrics, seamlessly blending with Elton's soulful melodies and impassioned performances.

In 1973, "Goodbye Yellow Brick Road" became a game-changer for the duo. The double album featured a plethora of hits, including "Bennie and the Jets," "Candle in the Wind," "Saturday Night's Alright for Fighting," and the title track "Goodbye Yellow Brick Road." Each song displayed Bernie's storytelling finesse, and the album's success propelled them to international stardom.

Their collaboration extended to film soundtracks as well. In 1975, they worked on "Captain Fantastic and the Brown Dirt Cowboy," a concept album recounting their early struggles and rise to fame. Meanwhile, "Don't Let the Sun Go Down on Me" from "Caribou" (1974) and "Sorry Seems to Be the Hardest Word" from "Blue Moves" (1976) further solidified their position as a force to be reckoned with in the music world.

The late 1970s saw the release of "Mama Can't Buy You Love" (1979), which became a top-ten hit in the United States, and "Empty Garden (Hey Hey Johnny)" (1982), a tribute to their late friend and musician John Lennon. Throughout the 1980s, Bernie and Elton continued to churn out hits such as "I'm Still Standing," "I Guess That's Why They Call It the Blues," and "Sad Songs (Say So Much)."

In 1994, they achieved unprecedented success with the soundtrack for Disney's "The Lion King." Bernie wrote the lyrics for the film's songs, including the Oscar-winning "Can You Feel the Love Tonight," which remains one of their most beloved and enduring hits. The soundtrack album became a massive commercial success and further expanded their reach to a new generation of fans.

In the new millennium, their partnership remained as vibrant as ever, with hits like "This Train Don't

Stop There Anymore" and "Electricity" (from the musical "Billy Elliot") captivating audiences worldwide. Their album "The Union" (2010), produced by T-Bone Burnett, earned critical acclaim and highlighted their continued creativity and relevance in the music industry.

The legacy of Bernie Taupin's songwriting success extends beyond the partnership with Elton John. He also collaborated with other artists, such as Alice Cooper, for whom he wrote the lyrics for the album "From the Inside" (1978), and Starship, with the hit "We Built This City" (1985).

Throughout his career, Bernie's lyrical brilliance garnered widespread recognition and admiration. He received numerous awards, including multiple Grammy Awards, a Tony Award for Best Original Score (for "Aida"), and induction into the Songwriters Hall of Fame.

Beyond accolades and awards, the enduring appeal of Bernie Taupin's songwriting lies in its ability to touch the hearts of listeners on a deep emotional level. His poetic storytelling, introspective themes, and powerful imagery have resonated with audiences worldwide, forging a connection that transcends time and cultural boundaries.

As a testament to their lasting impact, Bernie and Elton embarked on farewell tours, bidding farewell to their loyal fans while celebrating a musical legacy that spans over five decades. Bernie Taupin's songwriting success and the plethora of hits he co-created with Elton John have left an indelible mark on the music industry, shaping the very fabric of popular music and inspiring countless artists for generations to come.

PERSONAL LIFE AND RELATIONSHIPS

Bernie Taupin's personal life and relationships have been as intriguing and diverse as his songwriting. While he is widely known for his artistic collaboration with Elton John, he has led a private life away from the spotlight, which has been marked by various experiences and connections that have shaped him as an individual.

In his early years, Bernie Taupin embraced a bohemian lifestyle, often seeking solace and inspiration in the tranquility of nature. His upbringing in the English countryside left a lasting impact on his love for rural life and appreciation for the beauty of the natural world. This connection with nature is evident in many of his lyrics, which often evoke images of landscapes, seasons, and the ebb and flow of life.

During his rise to fame, Bernie experienced the whirlwind of success alongside Elton John. The adulation and fame that accompanied their hit records and sold-out concerts introduced him to a world that contrasted sharply with his rural roots. However, he managed to maintain a sense of grounding, often retreating to his countryside home to find peace and center himself amidst the frenzy of the music industry.

Bernie's romantic life has been an enigmatic aspect of his private persona. While he has been protective of his personal relationships, he has had a few notable partnerships. In 1971, he married Maxine Feibelman, a longtime friend, and they remained married for several years. However, the pressures of their respective careers ultimately led to their separation. Bernie and Maxine had two children together, daughters Aisha and Charley, who have remained an important part of his life.

In the late 1970s, Bernie met Heather Lynn Hodgins Kidd, an American artist, and they married in 1979. Their marriage brought more stability to Bernie's life, and they settled into a family-oriented life on a ranch in California. The couple also had two children, daughters Joanna and Ruby, further cementing Bernie's connection to family and home.

Bernie Taupin's personal life has not been without its share of challenges and setbacks. Like many artists, he faced moments of introspection and self-discovery, grappling with the demands of fame and artistic expression. However, through it all, he maintained a sense of authenticity and remained true to his artistic vision.

Outside of his songwriting partnership with Elton John, Bernie explored other artistic endeavors. He is an accomplished visual artist, expressing his creativity through painting and other forms of visual art. His art has been featured in galleries and exhibitions, showcasing another dimension of his artistic talents.

Throughout his life, Bernie has valued privacy, keeping a low profile in comparison to many other public figures. He has shied away from media attention and prefers to let his work speak for itself. This desire for a private life has allowed him to maintain a sense of balance and focus on his creative endeavors without the distraction of constant public scrutiny.

In recent years, Bernie Taupin has continued to collaborate with Elton John on new projects while also pursuing his own artistic ventures. His songwriting legacy remains firmly intact, with his lyrics continuing to resonate with audiences across the globe.

Overall, Bernie Taupin's personal life and relationships have been characterized by a deep appreciation for nature, a commitment to artistic expression, and a desire for privacy. While his collaboration with Elton John has defined much of his public identity, his personal journey has been a multifaceted exploration of creativity, family, and self-discovery. As he continues to navigate the ever-changing landscape of the music industry and artistic expression, Bernie Taupin's enigmatic presence and profound lyrical genius continue to captivate and inspire audiences worldwide.

ARTISTIC VENTURES BEYOND MUSIC

Beyond his illustrious music career, Bernie Taupin has delved into various artistic ventures, showcasing his creativity and versatility in multiple mediums. His artistic pursuits extend far beyond songwriting, and they provide a fascinating insight into the depth of his talent and artistic vision.

One of Bernie's significant artistic ventures has been his foray into the world of visual art. Throughout his life, he has maintained a passion for painting and drawing, using visual expression as another means to convey his emotions and creative ideas. His artistic style mirrors the evocative nature of his songwriting, often featuring bold and vibrant colors, abstract forms, and dreamlike landscapes. Bernie's paintings have been displayed in galleries around the world, giving admirers a chance to experience his artistry in a different form.

In the early 1980s, Bernie ventured into the realm of literature, penning a children's book titled "The Devil at High Noon." The book explores themes of friendship, courage, and environmental conservation through an imaginative narrative. Bernie's talent for storytelling shines through in this literary endeavor, demonstrating that his creative prowess extends beyond the world of music.

Another noteworthy artistic venture of Bernie Taupin was his collaboration with artist Mark Ryden for an exhibition titled "An Earwig of Consciousness" in 2007. The exhibit showcased Bernie's poetry and song lyrics alongside Ryden's intricate paintings, creating a fascinating blend of visual and written art that mesmerized audiences.

Moreover, Bernie Taupin's songwriting talents have found their way into the realm of theater. He teamed up with Elton John to create the music and lyrics for the Tony Award-winning musical "Aida" in 2000. The musical's success further solidified Bernie's reputation as a multi-faceted artist capable of excelling in various creative domains.

In recent years, Bernie has continued to explore artistic collaborations and ventures. He collaborated with artist Todd White on a series of art pieces titled "Butterflies and Bullets," which combined Bernie's poetry with White's visually arresting paintings. The exhibition offered audiences a unique fusion of poetry, visual art, and storytelling, further showcasing Bernie's artistic diversity.

Throughout his career, Bernie Taupin has remained committed to authenticity and creative expression, unafraid to experiment with different mediums and explore new artistic territories. His artistic ventures beyond music have allowed him to connect with audiences in fresh and innovative ways, showing that his creativity knows no bounds.

Beyond the spotlight and accolades, Bernie Taupin's artistic ventures exemplify his unyielding dedication to artistic exploration and self-expression. His willingness to push creative boundaries and embrace diverse art forms underscores his status as a true renaissance artist.

As Bernie Taupin's artistic journey continues, one thing remains abundantly clear: his boundless creativity and unwavering commitment to artistic expression will forever leave an indelible mark on the world of art and culture. Whether through his poetic lyrics, vibrant paintings, literary endeavors, or theatrical collaborations, Bernie Taupin's artistic ventures beyond music serve as a testament to the enduring power of creativity and the transformative impact of art on the human experience.

LEGACY AND IMPACT

Bernie Taupin's legacy and impact on the music industry are immeasurable. As the renowned lyricist and longtime collaborator of Sir Elton John, he has left an indelible mark on popular music. Taupin's poetic and thought-provoking lyrics have resonated with audiences worldwide, evoking emotions and connecting deeply with listeners.

His partnership with Elton John produced numerous timeless hits that have stood the test of time, such as "Your Song," "Rocket Man," and "Tiny Dancer." Taupin's ability to craft vivid and evocative imagery in his lyrics has earned him widespread admiration and critical acclaim.

Beyond his collaborations with Elton John, Bernie Taupin has worked with various other artists,

38

showcasing his versatility as a songwriter. His lyrical prowess has influenced generations of songwriters, inspiring them to explore new storytelling techniques and artistic expressions.

Moreover, Bernie Taupin's willingness to explore different themes and genres in his lyrics has made him an iconic figure in the music world. His work has transcended boundaries, reaching diverse audiences and leaving an everlasting impact on pop culture.

Beyond music, Taupin's influence extends into the realm of visual arts. As an accomplished painter and artist, he has showcased his creativity on canvas, further cementing his artistic legacy.

Bernie Taupin's legacy is one of artistic brilliance and creative exploration. His contribution to the world of music and art has inspired countless individuals and will continue to inspire generations to come. Through his poetic mastery, Taupin has touched the hearts of millions, leaving an enduring mark on the fabric of popular culture.

BERNIE TAUPIN TODAY

As of today, Bernie Taupin continues to be a prolific and influential figure in the world of music and art. Despite spending much of his life in the limelight due to his celebrated collaboration with Elton John, Bernie has managed to maintain a sense of privacy and authenticity in his personal and artistic pursuits.

His enduring partnership with Elton John remains strong, and they have continued to work together on various projects over the years. Their farewell tours in recent years, including "Farewell Yellow Brick Road," have allowed them to bid a grand farewell to their loyal fans while celebrating their remarkable musical legacy.

Bernie Taupin's songwriting remains as resonant as ever, with his lyrical compositions continuing to captivate audiences worldwide. His ability to craft emotionally charged and thought-provoking lyrics has been a hallmark of his career, and his words continue to touch the hearts of listeners across generations.

Beyond music, Bernie's artistic endeavors in visual art have also flourished. His paintings and artistic collaborations have garnered praise and attention from art enthusiasts and critics alike. His abstract and emotive style in visual art reflects his poetic sensibilities, creating a harmonious fusion of creative expression.

Moreover, Bernie's literary pursuits have also expanded. He has written poetry and explored writing beyond song lyrics, showcasing his versatility and passion for storytelling in various forms.

Despite his impressive accomplishments, Bernie Taupin remains down-to-earth and true to himself. He has shied away from the glitz and glamour of fame, choosing to lead a private life away from the media spotlight. This dedication to maintaining a sense of authenticity has allowed him to focus on his creative endeavors without distractions.

As a celebrated artist and songwriter, Bernie Taupin's influence extends far beyond his own work. His impact on the music industry has been immeasurable, inspiring countless songwriters and musicians to pursue their artistic visions with sincerity and passion.

In recent years, Bernie has also been involved in philanthropic endeavors, using his platform to support various charitable causes. His contributions to organizations and initiatives focused on arts education and conservation reflect his commitment to giving back to society and making a positive impact.

As Bernie Taupin continues to embrace his artistic journey, his legacy remains firmly intact. His work continues to resonate with audiences, and his artistry serves as a testament to the enduring power of creativity and the profound connection that music and art can create across cultures and generations.

While he may prefer to remain out of the spotlight, Bernie Taupin's influence and impact on the world of music and art are undeniable. As fans and admirers celebrate his body of work, one thing is certain: Bernie Taupin's artistic genius will continue to inspire and enrich the lives of those who are touched by his words, his art, and his enduring artistic legacy.

CONCLUSION

In conclusion, Bernie Taupin's life and artistic journey stand as a testament to the transformative power of creativity and the profound impact of authentic self-expression. From his humble beginnings in the English countryside to becoming one of the most celebrated lyricists in music history, Taupin's unwavering dedication to his craft and his artistic vision have left an indelible mark on the world of music and art.

His collaborative partnership with Elton John exemplifies the magic that can be created when two creative geniuses come together in perfect harmony. Their enduring musical legacy spans over five decades, captivating audiences worldwide with emotionally charged lyrics and captivating melodies that have transcended generations.

Beyond his songwriting prowess, Bernie Taupin's artistic ventures have showcased his versatility and passion for storytelling in various forms. From visual art to literature, he has explored new territories and pushed creative boundaries, leaving admirers enthralled by his multifaceted talents.

Despite his success and fame, Bernie Taupin has remained grounded and true to himself. His dedication to maintaining a private life has allowed him to focus on his creative pursuits without distractions, ensuring that his artistic integrity remains untainted by the pressures of celebrity.

As he continues to explore new artistic horizons and collaborate with fellow creatives, Bernie Taupin's legacy continues to grow, inspiring aspiring artists to follow their passions and embrace their unique voices. His ability to connect with audiences on a deep emotional level through his lyrics and art is a testament to the enduring power of artistic expression.

Bernie Taupin's impact on the music industry and the world of art is not confined to his own achievements; it extends to the countless individuals he has influenced and touched with his evocative words and creative endeavors.

In the grand tapestry of music and art, Bernie Taupin's legacy will forever hold a place of distinction. His songs will continue to be sung, his art will continue to be admired, and his creative spirit will continue to inspire generations to come. As we celebrate his journey and artistic contributions, one thing is certain: Bernie Taupin's imprint on the world of creativity is timeless, and his voice will forever echo in the hearts and minds of those who find solace, inspiration, and joy in his artistic genius.

Printed in Great Britain
by Amazon

32567851R00029